Have a Cool Yule

Merry Christmas  *from Will Bullas*

froglights...

 THE GREENWICH WORKSHOP PRESS

D1621502

 A GREENWICH WORKSHOP PRESS BOOK

Published by the Greenwich Workshop Press. One Greenwich Place, P.O. Box 875, Shelton, CT 06484. (203) 925-0131 or (800) 243-4246.

Library of Congress Cataloging-in-Publication Data
Bullas, Will, 1949-
      Have a Cool Yule : Merry Christmas from Will Bullas
         p. cm.
ISBN 0-86713-068-7 (alk. paper)
      1. Bullas, Will, 1949- 2. Christmas in art. 3. Animals in art. 4. American wit and humor,
Pictorial. I. Title

ND1839.B77 A4 2001b
759.13--dc21

                                    2001040304

Limited edition prints and canvas reproductions, and figurines based on Will Bullas' paintings, are available exclusively through The Greenwich Workshop, Inc. and its 1200 dealers in North America. Collectors interested in obtaining information on available releases and the location of their nearest dealer are requested to visit our website at **www.greenwichworkshop.com** or to write or call the publisher at the address above.

Jacket front: *a cool yule...*
Book design by Sheryl P. Kober
Printed in Singapore by Imago
First Printing 2001
1 2 3 4 5   04 03 02 01

Yule be Home (Laughing) for Christmas...

The Yuletide is all wrapped up in this classic Will Bullas interpretation of the holiday season. From a tabby's *catnip Christmas*…to the duck-billed Santa Claus, trimmed up like a tree in *Santa gets lit…*, whimsical Christmas cheer is delivered by a band of feathered, furry and slippery revelers. "Yule" be guaranteed a chuckle with this undeniably wacky perspective on the not-so-traditional fun of the holiday season.

the big green gift...

the christmas goose...

a christmas moose...

...undles
...joy...

dressed for the holidays...

polar pucker...

the elf...

catnip christmas...

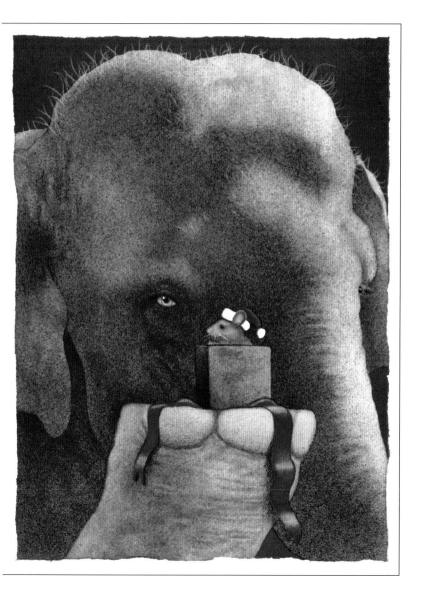

the best gifts
are friends...

bearing gifts...

the nutquacker...

moosletoad...

jingle this...

candy cane croaker...

holiday friends...

four calling birds...

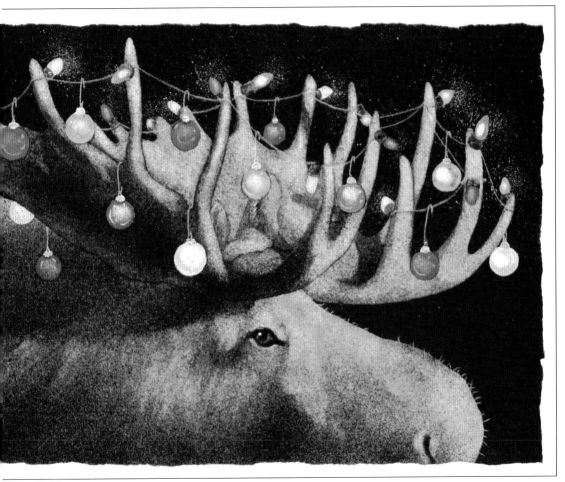

another christmas moose...

bearer of joy...

the christmas pudding...

the fiddler...

cool cracker...

a different kind of christmas...

the frog sled...

piggy santa...

santa gets lit...

a cool yule...

the mistletoad...

the
christmas
star...

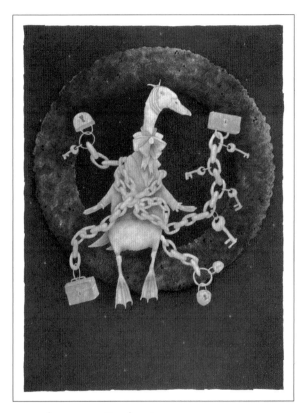

ghost of christmas past...

frog horn...

all I want
for christmas...

the
christmas
pug...

santa's hopper...

christmas
kisses and
holiday
hugs...